AMERIC. FOR B

A Comprehensive Guide to Rules, Strategies, and Techniques for Superior Play

Bernard A. Novak

COPYRIGHT PAGE

Table of Contents

Introduction

American football is one of the most thrilling and strategic sports on the planet, known for its physicality, teamwork, and fast-paced action. But with its complex rules, unique jargon, and various positions, it can be a bit overwhelming for beginners to fully grasp.

This book was created to simplify the game and help you not only understand it but enjoy it. Whether your goal is to start playing football, support your kids in youth leagues, or simply become a more informed fan, I've designed this guide to take you through every aspect of the sport. You'll start with the very basics—the rules, the field, and the essential skills—and move on to more advanced strategies and techniques. By the time you're done, you'll feel confident about your knowledge of the game, whether you're on the field, in the stands, or watching from the comfort of your home.

Why American Football?

American football is more than just a game; it's a cultural phenomenon, particularly in the United States. Every year, millions of fans tune in to watch the NFL, and youth leagues across the country fill up with aspiring athletes.

The game is also spreading internationally, with people from around the world becoming interested in the NFL, Super Bowl, and college football. Football is not only exciting to watch but also offers countless opportunities to learn valuable lessons about teamwork, perseverance, and strategy.

What You Will Learn

In this book, you'll get a step-by-step walkthrough of everything you need to know about the sport. Here's what you'll learn:

- The **fundamental rules** of football, broken down in a way that's easy to understand

- The **positions** and roles that each player takes on the field, from quarterbacks to linebackers

- Basic **strategies and plays** used by both offensive and defensive teams

- Essential **skills** you need to play, including how to catch, run, and tackle effectively

- Tips for improving your knowledge and enjoyment as a **spectator**

Whether you're stepping onto the field as a player or just want to feel more confident cheering from the stands, this book will give you the foundation you need to enjoy football to the fullest.

How to Use This Book

Each chapter of this book builds upon the previous one, starting with the basics and progressing toward a deeper understanding of the game. You can follow it in order or jump to sections that interest you most. If you're new to football, I recommend starting with the early chapters on rules, field layout, and positions to build a solid foundation. If you're more interested in strategy, skip ahead to the sections on offensive and defensive plays.

No matter how you use this book, the goal is to help you feel comfortable with the game. Whether you're on the sidelines, in the stands, or playing on the field, by the time you finish this guide, you'll be ready to enjoy football with confidence.

Chapter 1

The Basics of American Football

American football is a thrilling, fast-paced sport that combines athleticism, strategy, and teamwork. At first glance, it might seem complex, with its various positions, rules, and plays. But once you understand the core components of the game, you'll find that football is an exciting and highly rewarding sport to follow or play. In this chapter, we'll cover the essentials—the basic structure of the game, the objective, and key positions—so that you have a solid foundation to build on.

What Is American Football?

At its heart, American football is a team sport where two teams of eleven players each compete to score points by advancing the ball into the opposing team's end zone. The team with the most points at the end of the game wins. Points can be scored in various ways, such as by running the ball into the end zone (a touchdown) or kicking it through the opponent's goalposts (a field goal).

The game is played on a **rectangular field** with distinct markings, and the teams take turns playing on offense and defense. The offense attempts to move the ball down the field and score points, while the defense's goal is to stop the offense and prevent them from scoring. Teams also have specialized units for **special teams** plays, such as kickoffs and punts.

The Goal of the Game

In American football, the main goal is to score more points than the other team. A typical game consists of four quarters, each lasting 15 minutes, with a halftime break after the second quarter. The team that accumulates the most points by the end of the fourth quarter is declared the winner. In the event that there is a tie at the end of regulation time, the winner is decided in overtime.

There are two main ways to score points in football:

- **Touchdown (6 points)**: The offense scores a touchdown by getting the ball into the opponent's end zone, either by running or passing it.

- **Field Goal (3 points)**: The offense can also score points by kicking the ball through the opponent's goalposts.

- **Extra Points**: After a touchdown, the offense has the opportunity to earn additional points by either kicking the ball through the goalposts for one point or attempting another play from the two-yard line to score two points (known as a two-point conversion).

- **Safety (2 points)**: The defense can score if they tackle an offensive player with the ball in the offense's own end zone.

The team with the most points at the end of the game wins, and if there's a tie, special overtime rules are applied to determine the winner.

Key Positions and Roles

Each player on the football field has a specific position and role, and understanding these positions is crucial to grasping the flow of the game. The two main units on a football team are the **offense** and the **defense**, with special teams handling kicking situations.

Offensive Positions

The offensive team is responsible for advancing the ball down the field and scoring points. Here's a breakdown of the key offensive positions:

- **Quarterback (QB)**: The quarterback is the leader of the offense and the player who handles the ball most often. They call the plays, receive the snap from the center, and either pass the ball to a receiver, hand it off to a running back, or run with the ball themselves. A good quarterback must have a strong arm, quick decision-making skills, and the ability to read the defense.

- **Running Back (RB)**: The running back's primary job is to run with the ball after receiving it from the quarterback. They may also catch passes and block for other players. There are different types of running backs, including:

- o **Halfback (HB)**: A versatile runner and receiver.

- o **Fullback (FB)**: A powerful blocker who also runs with the ball occasionally.

- **Wide Receiver (WR)**: The wide receiver's main responsibility is to catch passes from the quarterback. They line up near the sideline and run specific routes to get open. Speed, agility, and good hands are critical for wide receivers.

- **Tight End (TE)**: A hybrid position between a receiver and a lineman, the tight end can catch passes but also blocks to support the running game. Tight ends need to be versatile, strong, and able to catch and block.

- **Offensive Linemen (OL)**: The offensive line consists of five players whose primary job is to protect the quarterback and block for the running back. These players are:

  - **Center (C)**: The center snaps the ball to the quarterback and is responsible for blocking defensive players.

  - **Guard (G)**: Guards line up on either side of the center and block for both the run and pass plays.

- o **Tackle (T)**: Tackles are the outermost linemen, blocking defensive ends and outside pass rushers.

Defensive Positions

The defense's job is to prevent the offense from scoring by tackling the ball carrier, intercepting passes, or forcing turnovers. Defensive positions include:

- **Defensive Linemen (DL)**: These players line up directly across from the offensive line and try to tackle the quarterback or stop the running back. Key positions include:

- ○ **Defensive End (DE)**: These players line up on the edges of the defensive line and aim to rush the passer or contain the outside run.

- ○ **Defensive Tackle (DT)**: These players line up in the middle of the defensive line and work to stop inside runs and pressure the quarterback.

- **Linebacker (LB)**: Linebackers play behind the defensive line and are involved in both stopping the run and defending against the pass. There are usually three or four linebackers, and they can blitz the quarterback or drop into coverage.

- **Cornerback (CB)**: Cornerbacks cover wide receivers and attempt to prevent them from catching passes. They play a critical role in pass defense and are often matched up one-on-one with the opposing team's best receiver.

- **Safety (S)**: Safeties are the last line of defense and play deep in the secondary to prevent long passes. There are typically two safeties:

  - **Free Safety (FS)**: Plays deep and covers the pass.

  - **Strong Safety (SS)**: Usually plays closer to the line of scrimmage and helps stop the run, but also covers passes.

The Flow of the Game

Each team takes turns playing **offense** and **defense**. The offense tries to move the ball down the field, while the defense aims to stop them. The offense gets **four downs** (or plays) to advance the ball at least **10 yards**. If they succeed, they earn a new set of four downs. If they fail, the other team takes possession of the ball. Here's how the game flows:

1. **Kickoff**: The game begins with a kickoff, where one team kicks the ball to the other. The receiving team attempts to return the ball as far down the field as possible.

2. **Offensive Drive**: Once the offense has the ball, their goal is to move down the field and score.

They have four downs to advance the ball at least 10 yards. If they succeed, they get a fresh set of downs.

3. **Turnovers and Punts**: If the offense fails to move 10 yards in four downs, they usually punt the ball to the other team, giving up possession. However, turnovers like interceptions (when a defender catches a pass intended for an offensive player) or fumbles (when the ball is dropped and recovered by the defense) can also give the defense the ball.

4. **Scoring**: The offense can score points by getting the ball into the end zone for a touchdown, or by kicking a field goal through the uprights. After a touchdown, they

can attempt an extra point or a two-point conversion.

5. **Switching Sides**: After each score, the scoring team kicks off to the other team, and the roles of offense and defense switch. This cycle repeats throughout the game.

Basic Football Terminology

Understanding the terms used in football is crucial for following the game. Here are some essential terms to get you started:

- **Snap**: The action of the center handing or passing the ball to the quarterback to start a play.

- **Down**: A play or attempt to move the ball. Offenses have four downs to advance 10 yards.

- **Line of Scrimmage**: The invisible line where the ball is placed at the start of each play.

- **Blitz**: A defensive tactic where extra players rush the quarterback in an attempt to sack him.

- **Sack**: When a defensive player tackles the quarterback behind the line of scrimmage, resulting in a loss of yards.

- **Interception**: When a defensive player catches a pass intended for an offensive player, gaining possession of the ball for their team.

Chapter 2

The Rules of the Game

American football has a set of structured rules that govern how it is played. From how the game is scored to how teams must advance the ball, every aspect of the game is defined by clear guidelines. For beginners, understanding the rules is essential for both playing and enjoying the game as a spectator. In this chapter, we will cover everything from the structure of a football game, how points are scored, to common penalties, and what happens during player substitutions.

Game Structure

An American football game is divided into four **quarters**, each lasting 15 minutes, with a **halftime break** after the second quarter. While the clock counts down during the game, it can stop and start depending on various situations, such as incomplete passes, players running out of bounds, penalties, or timeouts. Understanding the structure and timing of the game is fundamental to following the flow of the match.

Timing and Game Clock

- **Four Quarters**: The game is divided into four 15-minute quarters.

- **Halftime**: There is a 12-15 minute break between the second and third quarters.

- **Clock Management**: The game clock can stop for several reasons, including:

  o Incomplete passes

  o Running out of bounds

  o Timeouts (each team is allowed three timeouts per half)

  o Penalties and injuries

The team with the most points at the end of the fourth quarter wins. If the game is tied at the end of regulation, it enters **overtime**, where additional rules apply to determine a winner.

Overtime Rules

In the NFL, if the score is tied at the end of regulation, overtime consists of an additional period of 10 minutes. Here are the key overtime rules:

- The game starts with a **coin toss** to determine which team gets possession of the ball first.

- If the team receiving the ball scores a **touchdown** on its first possession, they win the game. If they only score a **field goal**, the other team gets a chance to score.

- If both teams have possession and the score is still tied after 10 minutes, the game ends in a tie (in regular-season NFL games). In playoff games, overtime continues until there is a winner.

In college football, the opponent's 25-yard line is where each team starts a possession. The game continues in extra periods until one team outscores the other.

Scoring

In football, there are several ways to score points. Teams can score through **touchdowns**, **field goals**, **extra points**, and **safeties**. Understanding how points are accumulated is crucial for understanding the game's strategy and objectives.

Touchdown (6 points)

A **touchdown** is the most valuable scoring play in football, worth 6 points. A touchdown occurs when the ball is either carried or caught in the opponent's **end zone**. Both running and passing plays can result in a touchdown.

- **Running Touchdown**: The ball carrier crosses the opponent's goal line while maintaining control of the ball.

- **Passing Touchdown**: A receiver catches a pass in the end zone or catches it outside the end zone and runs in for the score.

Extra Point (1 or 2 points)

After scoring a touchdown, the offense gets a chance to earn **extra points** in one of two ways:

- **Kick Extra Point (1 point)**: The team can kick the ball through the goalposts from the **2-yard**

line. This is the most common method and is worth one point.

- **Two-Point Conversion (2 points)**: Instead of kicking, the offense can attempt to run or pass the ball into the end zone again from the 2-yard line. Successfully completing this play earns the team two points.

Field Goal (3 points)

A **field goal** is worth 3 points and is typically attempted on fourth down if the offense is within range of the goalposts but unable to score a touchdown. To score a field goal, the kicker must successfully kick the ball through the opponent's goalposts.

Safety (2 points)

A **safety** occurs when the defense tackles an offensive player with the ball in the offense's own **end zone**, forcing the offense to lose possession in a dangerous area. The defense is awarded 2 points, and the offense must kick the ball to the opposing team after the safety. Safeties are relatively rare but can be game-changing events when they occur.

Downs and Yardage

The concept of **downs** and **yardage** is at the core of American football. The offense has **four downs** (or chances) to advance the ball at least **10 yards**. If they succeed, they are awarded another set of four downs. If they fail to advance 10 yards in four downs, they must either **punt** the ball to the opposing team or attempt a **field goal**, depending on their field position.

How Downs Work

- **First Down**: The offense begins with a first down and must move the ball 10 yards to earn another first down.

- **Second Down**: If the offense does not gain 10 yards on the first down, they have a second down to try again.

- **Third Down**: If the offense fails to gain 10 yards after two downs, they face a third down. On third down, the offense will often attempt a pass play to gain the remaining yards.

- **Fourth Down**: If the offense still has not gained 10 yards after three downs, they can either go for it (attempt to gain the needed yardage), punt the ball to the opposing team, or attempt a field goal (if close enough to the goalposts).

If the offense successfully gains 10 yards or more, they are awarded a **first down** and get a fresh set of four downs.

Penalties

Football is a physical game, but there are strict rules governing how players can engage with one another. When these rules are broken, **penalties** are called by the referees, and the offending team is punished with the loss of yardage or other consequences. Penalties can have a major impact on the game, changing field position, nullifying big plays, or giving a team another chance to continue their drive.

Common Penalties

Here are some of the most common penalties in football:

1. **Offside**: Before the ball is snapped, a defensive player crosses the line of scrimmage. The defense is assessed a 5-yard penalty as a result.

2. **False Start**: An offensive player moves before the ball is snapped. This results in a 5-yard penalty against the offense.

3. **Holding**: When a player illegally grabs or holds an opponent, preventing them from moving. Offensive holding results in a 10-yard penalty, while defensive holding results in a 5-yard penalty and an automatic first down.

4. **Pass Interference**: When a player makes illegal contact with a receiver attempting to catch a pass. Defensive pass interference results in the offense being awarded the ball at the spot of the foul, and an automatic first down.

5. **Roughing the Passer**: When a defensive player hits the quarterback after the ball has been thrown, resulting in a 15-

yard penalty and an automatic first down.

6. **Personal Foul**: A severe violation, often involving unnecessary roughness or dangerous play. This results in a 15-yard penalty and an automatic first down.

Penalty Enforcement

When a penalty is called, referees throw a yellow flag to indicate the infraction. The **yardage** of the penalty depends on the severity of the foul and the nature of the penalty. Most penalties result in a loss of 5, 10, or 15 yards, depending on the infraction. In some cases, penalties also result in an **automatic first down** for the offense, or the loss of a down.

Player Substitutions

Football is unique in that it allows **unlimited substitutions** between plays. Teams are constantly rotating players in and out of the game based on the situation, play type, and strategy. There are specific units for offense, defense, and special teams, and players on each unit specialize in their particular role.

When and How Substitutions Occur

- **Between Plays**: Substitutions can occur after the whistle is blown and before the next play begins. Coaches will often send in different players depending on the down and distance, or if they expect a running or passing play.

- **Situational Substitutions**: For example, a team may substitute defensive linemen for smaller, faster players if they expect the offense to pass the ball.

There are no limits to the number of substitutions a team can make, which allows for dynamic game management and the use of specialized personnel.

The Kickoff and Possession Changes

Football begins with a **kickoff**, where one team kicks the ball to the other team to start the game. Kickoffs also occur after a team scores, to give possession to the other team. There are a few key concepts related to kickoffs and possession changes:

- **Kickoff**: The team kicking off sends the ball to the other team, which attempts to return it as far down the field as possible. The receiving team's offense starts their drive from where the ball is downed or where the return ends.

- **Punts**: If the offense fails to gain a first down, they can **punt** the ball to the opposing team on fourth down, which helps shift field position in their favor. The opposing team then gets possession and starts their offensive drive.

- **Turnovers**: If the defense forces a **turnover**, such as an **interception** or a **fumble**, they immediately gain possession of the ball and take over on offense.

Special Teams

Special teams play a crucial role in football during kickoffs, punts, and field goal attempts. Special teams units consist of players who specialize in kicking and returning the ball, blocking kicks, or tackling returners. Special teams plays can have a significant impact on field position and can even result in points, such as through a field goal or a kickoff return for a touchdown.

Game Strategies and Key Concepts

While understanding the rules is critical, football is as much about **strategy** as it is about physical skill. Teams must decide how to use their four downs, manage the game clock, and use field position to their advantage. Offenses may choose to run the ball to control the clock and wear down the defense, while defenses may blitz to pressure the quarterback into making mistakes.

Key strategic concepts include:

- **Field Position**: Teams aim to maintain favorable field position, starting their offensive drives closer to the opponent's end zone.

- **Clock Management**: In close games, managing the game clock becomes critical. Teams may run the ball more to keep the clock moving or call timeouts to preserve time for a final drive.

- **Play Calling**: Coaches design plays based on their players' strengths and the weaknesses of the opposing defense. Offenses use a mix of running and passing plays to keep the defense guessing, while defenses adjust to counter the offense's tactics.

Chapter 3

Understanding the Field and Equipment

American football is a sport deeply connected to its playing environment and the specialized equipment players use. To fully grasp the intricacies of the game, it's essential to understand both the layout of the field and the specific gear that protects the players and helps them perform at their best. In this chapter, we will explore the dimensions of the field, the key zones and markings, as well as the protective and performance-enhancing equipment used by players.

The Football Field: Dimensions and Key Zones

A standard American football field is 120 yards long and 53.3 yards wide. While the field's structure may seem straightforward, there are many important zones, lines, and markings that have specific functions and affect how the game is played.

Field Dimensions and Layout

- **Length**: The field is 100 yards long between the two **goal lines**, with an additional 10-yard **end zone** on each side, making the total length 120 yards.

- **Width**: The field is 53.3 yards (160 feet) wide.

- **End Zones**: The areas beyond the goal lines are called the end zones. These are crucial for scoring touchdowns. Each team defends one end zone and tries to advance the ball into the opponent's end zone to score.

Field Markings and Lines

1. **Goal Lines**: The two goal lines are located 100 yards apart, marking the boundary between the main playing field and the end zones. A team must cross the opponent's goal line with the ball to score a touchdown.

2. **Yard Lines**: Horizontal white lines cross the field every 5 yards, helping players, referees, and viewers identify how far the

ball has been moved. Every yard is also marked by smaller tick marks, which are used to measure precise progress.

3. **Hash Marks**: The hash marks are short lines running parallel to the sidelines, spaced 1 yard apart and 70 feet 9 inches from each sideline. They are used to mark the ball's placement after a play ends, depending on where the previous play stopped.

4. **50-Yard Line**: This is the center of the field, dividing the territory between the two teams. When the offense crosses this line, they are said to be in **opponent territory**.

5. **Goalposts**: Positioned at the back of each end zone, goalposts are used for **field goals** and **extra points**. The two vertical posts are 10 feet tall and are 18 feet 6 inches apart in professional and college football, while high school goalposts are slightly wider at 23 feet 4 inches apart.

6. **Sidelines**: The long boundary lines running the length of the field are known as the sidelines. A player is considered "out of bounds" when they step on or beyond these lines.

7. **End Lines**: The lines marking the back of the end zones are called the end lines. Any ball that goes beyond these lines is out of

bounds, and plays are stopped at that point.

Key Zones of the Field

Each area of the football field has strategic importance, and teams employ different tactics depending on where they are positioned:

- **Red Zone**: The area between the opponent's 20-yard line and the goal line is known as the "red zone." Scoring becomes highly probable in this zone, but the defense is often more aggressive here.

- **Midfield**: Around the 50-yard line is the midfield area, which is crucial for field position. Teams aim to push into their opponent's half to reduce the distance to the end zone.

- **End Zone**: The most critical zone of the field, where touchdowns are scored. A team must carry the ball into or catch it in the end zone to secure 6 points.

- **Goal Line**: Defensively, the goal line is the last line of defense. Offensively, crossing it with the ball means a touchdown.

Football Equipment: A Player's Armor

American football is a full-contact sport, and because of the high level of physicality, players must wear protective gear. The equipment is designed to prevent injuries while allowing players to move, block, tackle, and perform at their best.

Helmet

The **football helmet** is the most recognizable and important piece of equipment. It protects the head from concussions and other injuries.

- **Shell**: The outer layer, usually made of polycarbonate plastic, absorbs impact during collisions.

- **Face Mask**: A metal cage attached to the helmet to protect the face while still allowing for visibility.

- **Chin Strap**: Keeps the helmet securely in place. A well-fitted chin strap is crucial to prevent the helmet from shifting during play.

- **Visor (optional)**: Some players use a clear or tinted plastic visor attached to the face mask to protect their eyes from glare or injury.

Modern helmets are equipped with **advanced padding and cushioning** to reduce the risk of head injuries, including concussions. Some helmets also have sensors to monitor impact levels during games.

Shoulder Pads

The next critical piece of equipment is the **shoulder pads**, which protect the upper body. These pads are built with **hard plastic shells** and padded insides to absorb shocks from hits, tackles, and falls.

- **Front and Back Plates**: The shoulder pads extend to cover the chest, shoulders, and upper back.

- **Straps**: Adjustable straps secure the pads around the player's torso, ensuring a snug fit.

- **Variety by Position**: Different positions require different styles of shoulder pads. For example, wide receivers and quarterbacks use lighter, more flexible shoulder pads to maintain mobility, while linemen use heavier pads for more protection.

Jersey

Over the shoulder pads, players wear a **football jersey** made of durable, flexible fabric that fits tightly to prevent opponents from grabbing onto it.

Jerseys display the team's colors, logo, and the player's number. The tight fit is essential for performance and safety, as it reduces the risk of being pulled down by the jersey during tackles.

Pants

Football pants come equipped with slots for additional padding. They are tight-fitting, just like jerseys, and include pockets for protective gear.

- **Hip Pads**: Protect the hip bones from contact and tackles.

- **Thigh Pads**: Cover the upper thighs and help shield against impacts during collisions.

- **Knee Pads**: Provide protection for the knees, especially during falls or low tackles.

Cleats

Football cleats are specially designed shoes with studs on the soles to give players **traction** on grass or artificial turf. Proper cleats prevent slipping and help players make quick cuts, accelerate, and stop abruptly. Cleats come in different types, including **low-cut**, **mid-cut**, and **high-top** varieties, depending on the position and personal preference.

- **Low-Cut Cleats**: Provide maximum mobility and are popular among wide receivers and defensive backs.

- **Mid-Cut Cleats**: Offer a balance between mobility and ankle support, commonly used by running backs and linebackers.

- **High-Top Cleats**: Provide the most ankle support, often worn by linemen who need stability while blocking or rushing.

Gloves

While not mandatory, many football players wear **gloves** for better grip, especially in wet or cold conditions. There are different types of gloves depending on the position:

- **Receiver Gloves**: Designed with sticky, tacky palms to help wide receivers catch the ball.

- **Linemen Gloves**: Heavier and padded to protect hands during blocking and tackling.

- **Quarterback Gloves**: Some quarterbacks use gloves on their non-throwing hand for a better grip while handling the ball.

Mouthguard

The **mouthguard** is a small, but vital, piece of equipment that protects a player's teeth and jaw from injury during contact. Most players attach their mouthguards to their helmets to prevent losing them during play.

Other Padding

In addition to shoulder pads and pants padding, players often wear other types of protective gear, especially for high-impact positions.

- **Rib Protectors**: These pads protect the ribs and abdomen, especially useful for quarterbacks and wide receivers.

- **Neck Rolls and Collars**: Linemen and linebackers sometimes wear extra padding around their necks for protection against whiplash or severe impacts.

- **Elbow Pads**: Some players use padded sleeves or pads to protect their elbows during falls.

The Football

The football itself is a key part of the game, and it's carefully designed for performance. An official football used in the NFL is made of **cowhide leather** and weighs about 14-15 ounces. It is an oblong, elliptical shape, which allows for better aerodynamic properties, especially when thrown in a spiral.

- **Size and Weight**: The standard length of a football is 11 inches, with a circumference of about 22 inches at its widest point.

- **Laces**: The football's laces allow quarterbacks to grip the ball securely when throwing. Kickers also use the laces for control during kicks.

- **Inflation**: The ball must be inflated to a pressure of 12.5-13.5 pounds per square inch (PSI) to ensure optimal performance. In 2015, the **Deflategate** controversy highlighted the importance of proper inflation levels in competitive play.

Football sizes vary depending on the level of play:

- **Youth Football**: Slightly smaller and lighter than the professional ball.

- **High School and College Football**: Slightly larger than youth footballs, but smaller than the NFL version.

Special Teams Equipment

Special teams play an essential role in football, particularly during kickoffs, punts, and field goals. For these plays, some equipment becomes critical:

- **Kicking Tee**: Used for kickoffs, the **kicking tee** elevates the ball slightly off the ground, helping the kicker achieve greater height and distance.

- **Holder**: During field goal attempts, a **holder** kneels on the field and holds the ball upright for the kicker to strike. This is usually done without a tee in the NFL and college football.

- **Long Snapper Equipment**: A **long snapper** is a player who specializes in snapping the ball over longer distances, especially for punts and field goals. Their gloves and protective equipment are crucial to ensure precision and safety during snaps.

Chapter 4

Offensive Strategies and Plays

In American football, the offense's goal is to advance the ball down the field and score points, either by reaching the end zone for a touchdown or by kicking a field goal. To achieve this, offensive teams develop strategies and employ a wide variety of plays designed to outmaneuver the defense. These plays are based on team strengths, opponent weaknesses, and game situations. In this chapter, we will dive into the core offensive strategies, break down the types of plays that teams run, and explore how offensive coordinators craft game plans to create scoring opportunities.

Offensive Philosophy: Controlling the Game

The primary objective of any offense is to move the ball effectively and maintain possession long enough to score points. The most successful offenses are those that can control both the pace and tempo of the game. To do this, teams must choose an offensive strategy that suits their personnel and fits within the context of the game. Offensive philosophies can be broken down into three primary approaches:

1. **Run-Oriented Offense**

    o Teams that emphasize the running game seek to control the clock, wear down the defense, and keep their offense on the field for extended periods. These teams rely on a powerful offensive line and skilled running backs to consistently gain yardage on the ground.

- **Pros**: Effective running offenses are difficult to stop when they can consistently gain yardage and control the clock. They also minimize the risk of turnovers, as running plays are less likely to result in interceptions.

- **Cons**: A run-heavy offense can be predictable, and if stopped early in downs, teams are forced into longer yardage situations on third down.

2. **Pass-Oriented Offense**

- ○ Pass-heavy teams focus on gaining yardage through the air, utilizing their quarterback and wide receivers to exploit mismatches and stretch the defense vertically. This strategy often relies on precision passing and quick decision-making by the quarterback.

- ○ **Pros**: Passing offenses can generate large chunks of yardage quickly and can be especially effective when trailing, allowing teams to cover long distances in a short period of time.

- o **Cons**: Passing the ball more frequently can lead to higher turnover risks (interceptions) and greater exposure to quarterback pressure from opposing defenses.

3. **Balanced Offense**

   - o A balanced offensive attack incorporates both running and passing plays in roughly equal measure. This approach aims to keep the defense guessing, making it more difficult for them to anticipate the next move.

- Pros: Balanced offenses are less predictable, allowing them to adjust based on game flow and take advantage of both run and pass defenses.

- Cons: While balanced, this approach requires a well-rounded roster, and teams may struggle if they don't have equally skilled personnel for both running and passing plays.

The choice between these philosophies depends on factors like the team's quarterback strength, running back talent, offensive line quality, and coaching philosophy.

Offensive Formations

Before any play can unfold, the offense must line up in a formation that sets the stage for the play. Formations dictate how the offense will attack the defense and are based on how players are positioned on the field. The primary players involved are the **quarterback**, **running backs**, **wide receivers**, and **tight ends**, who line up behind the **offensive line**.

Basic Offensive Formations

1. **Pro Set Formation**

- ○ This formation is a balanced setup with two running backs (one fullback, one halfback) behind the quarterback, two wide receivers, and a tight end.

71

It is versatile and allows for both running and passing plays.

2. **I-Formation**

  o Named for the vertical alignment of the quarterback, fullback, and halfback, the I-Formation is a run-heavy formation. The fullback acts as a lead blocker for the halfback, making it ideal for powerful, straight-ahead running plays.

3. **Shotgun Formation**

  o In the shotgun formation, the quarterback lines up several yards behind the center, giving them more time to read the defense before receiving the ball. This formation is often used for passing plays but can also incorporate runs and draws.

4. **Single Back (Ace) Formation**

   o The single back formation eliminates the fullback, leaving only one running back behind the quarterback. This allows for more wide receivers or tight ends to be added to the play, making it a versatile formation for both passing and running.

5. **Spread Formation**

- The spread formation involves spreading wide receivers across the field to "spread out" the defense, creating gaps in coverage. It is heavily used in passing offenses and is designed to exploit defensive mismatches and coverage breakdowns.

Personnel Groupings

Formations also rely on personnel groupings, which refer to the number of running backs, tight ends, and wide receivers on the field. These groupings affect how the defense aligns itself and responds to the offense's formation.

- **11 Personnel**: 1 running back, 1 tight end, and 3 wide receivers.

This is the most common personnel grouping in modern football, allowing for balanced run and pass options.

- **12 Personnel**: 1 running back and 2 tight ends. This formation is commonly used for run-heavy plays or short-yardage situations, but it can also create favorable mismatches for play-action passes.

- **21 Personnel**: 2 running backs and 1 tight end. This grouping often emphasizes the power running game, but teams can also use it to set up passing plays by sending running backs into pass routes.

Types of Offensive Plays

Now that we've explored the basic formations and strategies, let's break down the different types of offensive plays that teams use to advance the ball. Offensive plays fall into two main categories: **running plays** and **passing plays**.

Running Plays

Running plays are designed to move the ball by handing it off to a running back, who attempts to gain yards by evading defenders. Success in the running game often hinges on strong blocking from the offensive line and effective use of **lead blockers**.

1. **Dive Play**

   o The dive play is a straightforward run where

the running back takes the handoff and runs directly up the middle between the offensive guards. It is designed to gain short yardage and is often used in power-running situations.

2. Off-Tackle Run

- In an off-tackle run, the running back runs toward the outside of the offensive line, aiming for a gap between the offensive tackle and the tight end. This play allows the back to avoid the congested middle of the defense and find open space on the edge.

3. Sweep

o A sweep play involves the running back moving parallel to the line of scrimmage toward the sideline before turning upfield. The offensive linemen or lead blockers "pull" (move laterally) to create blocking lanes outside the formation.

4. **Draw Play**

o The draw is a deceptive running play that begins by mimicking a passing play. The quarterback drops back as if to pass, then hands the ball to the running back, who runs through the gaps created by the defense's retreat into pass coverage.

5. **Option Run**

- o In an option play, the quarterback has the choice to either hand the ball off to the running back or keep it and run themselves, depending on how the defense reacts. This is commonly used in mobile quarterback systems.

Passing Plays

Passing plays involve the quarterback throwing the ball to a receiver, tight end, or running back. These plays can be short, intermediate, or long passes, depending on the situation and the defense's alignment.

1. **Slant Route**

- In a slant route, the receiver runs a short route angled inward across the field. This route is effective for quick, short-yardage completions and can exploit defenses in man-to-man coverage.

2. **Go Route (Fly Route)**

- The go route is a deep passing play where the receiver runs straight down the field, attempting to beat the defender with speed. This route is often used to stretch the defense and create big-play opportunities.

3. **Post Route**

o On a post route, the receiver runs vertically for 10-15 yards before cutting toward the middle of the field at a 45-degree angle. This is a deep passing play designed to attack the "post" area of the field between the safeties.

4. **Screen Pass**

o The screen pass is designed to neutralize aggressive defensive pressure. The quarterback quickly throws a short pass to a receiver or running back behind the line of scrimmage while the offensive linemen "screen" or block defenders in front of the ball carrier.

5. **Play-Action Pass**

- In a play-action pass, the offense fakes a handoff to the running back to make the defense believe it's a run play. The quarterback then pulls the ball back and throws to a receiver downfield. Play-action passes are effective at drawing defenders out of position, particularly in run-heavy situations.

6. **Hail Mary**

- The Hail Mary is a desperation deep pass, typically used at the end of a half or game when time is running out. The quarterback throws the ball as far as possible toward a group of receivers near the end zone, hoping for a catch.

RPO (Run-Pass Option)

In recent years, the **RPO (Run-Pass Option)** has become a popular offensive concept, especially at the collegiate and professional levels. In an RPO play, the quarterback has the option to either hand the ball off for a run, keep it and run themselves, or throw a quick pass, depending on the defense's reaction.

- **How it Works**: The offensive line blocks as if it's a run play, but the quarterback reads a specific defender (often a linebacker or

83

defensive end) to decide whether to hand off the ball or pass it.

- **Advantages**: The RPO is difficult for defenses to predict because it offers multiple potential outcomes on a single play.

Developing an Offensive Game Plan

The best offenses don't rely on a single strategy or play. They mix different plays and formations to keep the defense off balance and constantly guessing. Offensive coordinators spend hours studying opposing defenses to identify weaknesses and tendencies that can be exploited. A well-rounded game plan includes:

1. **First-Down Plays**: Choosing plays that put the team in favorable second-down situations, often aiming for short, manageable gains.

2. **Third-Down Plays**: Crafting plays that target the yardage needed for first downs, using short passes or runs based on the defense's tendencies.

3. **Red Zone Strategy**: Special plays designed for scoring opportunities within 20 yards of the end zone, where the field becomes more compressed, and defenses tighten.

4. **Two-Minute Offense**: A fast-paced, no-huddle offense designed to move the ball quickly

down the field, particularly at the
end of a half or game.

Chapter 5

Defensive Strategies and Plays

In American football, defense is all about stopping the offense from advancing the ball, forcing turnovers, and limiting scoring opportunities. A great defense can dominate a game, forcing the opposing offense into mistakes and dictating the pace of play. Defensive strategies vary based on the type of offense they face, but the ultimate goal remains the same: disrupt the opponent's game plan. In this chapter, we will explore defensive philosophies, formations, common strategies, and the various plays defenses use to counter the offense.

Defensive Philosophy: Control and Disrupt

The defense's job is to control the pace of the game by limiting the offensive team's ability to score. There are several key principles that guide defensive strategies:

1. **Limit Yardage**: Prevent the offense from moving the ball down the field by stopping running plays and disrupting passing routes.

2. **Create Turnovers**: Force mistakes like fumbles and interceptions to regain possession of the ball for the offense.

3. **Pressure the Quarterback**: Apply constant pressure on the

quarterback to force hurried throws, sacks, or poor decisions.

4. **Force Negative Plays**: Tackling players for loss of yardage or forcing incompletions sets up difficult down-and-distance situations for the offense.

A well-coached defense is both reactive and proactive, reading offensive formations and adjusting their own alignments accordingly. Defenses need to anticipate offensive tendencies while being flexible enough to adapt on the fly.

Defensive Formations

The first step in any defensive play is determining the defensive formation. The defensive formation sets the foundation for how the team will align players to cover the field, stop runs, and defend against passes. Just like offensive formations, defensive formations depend on the personnel, game situation, and the offensive formation they are facing.

Basic Defensive Formations

1. **4-3 Defense**

   o This is one of the most common defensive formations in football, featuring four defensive linemen and three linebackers. The four linemen (two defensive ends and two defensive tackles) focus on stopping the run and pressuring the quarterback, while the three linebackers provide support in both the run and pass defense.

- o **Strengths**: Solid balance between run and pass defense; allows linebackers to cover running backs or tight ends.

- o **Weaknesses**: Can struggle against spread offenses with multiple wide receivers.

2. **3-4 Defense**

- o In this formation, there are three defensive linemen and four linebackers. The extra linebacker provides additional flexibility in pass coverage or blitzing. This defense is often used by teams with strong linebackers.

- o **Strengths**: Increased versatility in blitz packages and pass coverage; disguises where pressure is coming from.

- o **Weaknesses**: Requires very strong and athletic defensive linemen to occupy blockers.

3. Nickel Defense

- o The nickel defense is used primarily to defend against passing plays. It removes one linebacker and adds an extra defensive back, often referred to as the "nickelback." The goal is to cover additional wide receivers in passing situations.

- o **Strengths**: Better coverage against multiple wide receiver sets.

- o **Weaknesses**: Weaker against the run because of the reduced number of linebackers.

4. **Dime Defense**

- o The dime defense takes the nickel concept further by replacing another linebacker with a sixth defensive back. It's used almost exclusively in obvious passing situations or at the end of a game to defend against a long passing play.

- ○ **Strengths**: Strong coverage against deep passing plays.

- ○ **Weaknesses**: Extremely vulnerable to running plays.

Hybrid Defenses

Some teams employ hybrid defensive formations, blending elements of the 4-3 and 3-4 defenses. A common hybrid is the **4-2-5 defense**, which uses four linemen, two linebackers, and five defensive backs. These formations allow defenses to remain flexible and adjust to offensive trends, such as the increasing use of spread formations and fast-paced offenses.

Defensive Roles and Responsibilities

Each position on the defense plays a specific role, whether it's stopping the run, covering receivers, or rushing the quarterback. Let's break down the responsibilities of each position:

1. **Defensive Line**: The defensive line's job is to stop the run and put pressure on the quarterback. The defensive ends are usually responsible for containing the outside edge of the line, while the defensive tackles focus on plugging up the middle and collapsing the pocket.

   o **Defensive Ends (DE)**: These players line up on the outside of the defensive line and are tasked with rushing the quarterback and setting the edge to contain outside runs.

- ○ **Defensive Tackles (DT)**: Positioned in the middle of the defensive line, these players are responsible for stopping inside runs and pushing back offensive linemen to disrupt the backfield.

2. **Linebackers**: Linebackers are the heart of the defense, providing support in both the running and passing game. Depending on the defensive scheme, they may be asked to blitz the quarterback, cover tight

ends or running backs, or stop the run.

- **Middle Linebacker (MLB)**: Also known as the "Mike" linebacker, this player is often the leader of the defense, responsible for reading the offense and making adjustments. The MLB is primarily tasked with stopping the run and covering short-to-intermediate passes.

- **Outside Linebackers (OLB)**: Outside linebackers (often referred to as "Will" and "Sam") play on the edges of the defense. One OLB might be used to rush the quarterback (especially in a 3-4 defense), while the other may cover running backs or tight ends in pass coverage.

3. **Defensive Backs**: The primary role of defensive backs is to defend against the pass. These players cover wide receivers, defend deep passes, and attempt to intercept the ball. The defensive backs include both cornerbacks and safeties.

  ○ **Cornerbacks (CB)**: Cornerbacks line up opposite the wide receivers and are responsible for covering them on pass routes. They must have quick reaction times and good ball skills to prevent completions or force interceptions.

- **Safeties (S)**: Safeties (both free and strong) play deep in the defensive backfield and are the last line of defense. The **free safety (FS)** typically covers the deep middle of the field, while the **strong safety (SS)** supports the run and covers tight ends or slot receivers.

Defensive Strategies

Defensive coordinators use a variety of strategies and schemes to counter offensive plays. Defensive strategies are built around stopping the opponent's strengths and forcing them into uncomfortable situations.

Man-to-Man Coverage

In **man-to-man coverage**, each defensive back or linebacker is assigned to cover a specific offensive player, typically a wide receiver, tight end, or running back. This coverage scheme is effective against teams that rely on individual matchups. The defense relies on each player winning their individual battle.

- **Strengths**: Man coverage is excellent against short-to-intermediate passing routes because defenders can stay close to their assigned receiver.

- **Weaknesses**: If a defender loses their one-on-one matchup, it can lead to big plays. Man coverage also struggles against mobile quarterbacks who can scramble out of the pocket.

Zone Coverage

In **zone coverage**, defenders are responsible for specific areas of the field, rather than individual offensive players. The goal is to cover passing lanes and force the quarterback into difficult throws.

- **Strengths**: Zone coverage is useful for defending against deep passing plays and preventing long gains. It also allows defenders to keep their eyes on the quarterback, increasing the chances of interceptions.

- **Weaknesses**: Zone coverage can be vulnerable to quick, short passes that find gaps between zones. If the defense doesn't communicate well, receivers can slip into open areas for easy completions.

Blitzing

A **blitz** is when the defense sends more players than usual to rush the quarterback. This tactic is designed to overwhelm the offensive line and force the quarterback to make quick decisions, leading to sacks or turnovers. Defensive coordinators often disguise their blitzes to keep the offense guessing.

- **Strengths**: Blitzing can force the quarterback into rushed throws, sacks, and mistakes, disrupting the offensive flow.

- **Weaknesses**: Blitzing leaves fewer defenders in pass coverage, making the defense vulnerable to quick passes or big plays if the quarterback gets the ball out in time.

Common Defensive Plays

1. **Cover 2**

   o In the **Cover 2** scheme, the two safeties divide the deep part of the field into two zones, while the cornerbacks and linebackers cover the short and intermediate areas. This play is often used against

103

passing teams to limit deep throws.

- o **Strengths**: Effective at preventing long completions and forcing the offense to settle for shorter gains.

- o **Weaknesses**: Can be vulnerable to plays in the middle of the field, especially if the safeties are forced to cover too much ground.

2. **Cover 3**

- o In a **Cover 3** defense, the deep part of the field is divided into three zones, typically covered by the two cornerbacks and one safety. The remaining defenders cover the short zones and middle of the field.

- **Strengths**: Provides strong coverage against deep passes while maintaining some presence against the run.

- **Weaknesses**: The flat areas near the sidelines can be vulnerable to quick passes.

3. **Tampa 2**

- The **Tampa 2** is a variation of the Cover 2 defense, where the middle linebacker drops deep into pass coverage to cover the middle of the field. This scheme is designed to defend both the deep ball and intermediate passes.

- o **Strengths**: Covers deep routes and takes away passes to the middle of the field.

- o **Weaknesses**: Requires athletic linebackers to drop back in coverage, which can leave the defense vulnerable to the run.

4. **Blitz Packages**

- o **Zone Blitz**: A combination of zone coverage and a blitz, where defenders who are not rushing the quarterback drop into coverage. The idea is to confuse the offense and force quick decisions.

- **Man Blitz**: This blitz leaves defensive backs in man-to-man coverage while extra defenders rush the quarterback.

Chapter 6

Special Teams and Their Role

Special teams are one of the three key phases of American football, alongside offense and defense. While often overlooked by casual fans, special teams play a crucial role in determining field position, scoring opportunities, and game momentum. Special teams involve all plays that occur during kicks, punts, and returns, making them a high-stakes part of the game where a single mistake or big play can drastically affect the outcome.

This chapter will delve into the role of special teams, the key plays that occur in special teams scenarios, and the players who make up these units. Understanding special teams will give you insight into how teams manage field position, score extra points, and execute game-changing plays.

The Importance of Special Teams

Special teams play a pivotal role in determining the flow and outcome of a football game. Teams that excel in special teams often gain a significant advantage in field position, which can be the difference between scoring and punting. Special teams units also create opportunities for scoring through field goals, extra points, and returns, while also serving as a critical part of defending against big plays by the opposing team.

Key reasons why special teams are vital to the game include:

1. **Field Position**: Successful punts, kickoffs, and returns can dramatically shift field position, setting up the offense in favorable situations or pinning the opponent deep in their own territory.

2. **Scoring Opportunities**: Special teams are responsible for putting points on the board through field goals and extra points. A strong kicker can give a team confidence in close games, while a returner can score touchdowns on kick or punt returns.

3. **Momentum Swings**: A blocked punt, a long return, or a missed

field goal can completely shift the momentum of a game, giving one team an emotional and strategic advantage.

4. **Game-Changing Plays**: Special teams often involve high-risk, high-reward plays. A single mistake or big play—whether it's a muffed punt, a blocked kick, or a kickoff returned for a touchdown—can dramatically alter the outcome of a game.

Key Special Teams Plays

There are several key types of plays that involve special teams, each of which serves a unique purpose in the game. These include kickoffs, punts, field goals, extra points, and returns.

Kickoffs

The kickoff occurs at the start of each half and after a team scores. The kicking team lines up on the 35-yard line, and the kicker's job is to kick the ball as deep into the opponent's territory as possible. The goal is to force the opposing team to start their offensive drive from a less favorable position.

- **Kickoff Coverage**: The kicking team must rush down the field and tackle the returner before they can gain significant yardage. Strong kickoff coverage is crucial to prevent long returns and keep the opponent deep in their own territory.

- **Kickoff Return**: The return team attempts to gain as many yards as possible by catching the ball and running it back. Special return plays are designed to block the coverage unit and create open lanes for the returner to advance the ball.

- **Touchback**: A touchback occurs when the kickoff lands in the end zone and the returner does not attempt to run it out. The ball is then placed at the 25-yard line, and the offense starts their drive from there. Kickers often aim for touchbacks to prevent long returns.

Punts

Punting is used when the offense fails to get a first down and is too far from the end zone to attempt a field goal. The punter kicks the ball downfield, ideally forcing the receiving team to start their next drive as far from the end zone as possible.

- **Punt Coverage**: The goal of the punt coverage team is to stop the returner from gaining many yards after the punt. Effective coverage involves sprinting down the field to tackle the returner quickly or forcing a fair catch.

- **Punt Return**: The return team's job is to set up blocks to allow the punt returner to gain yards after catching the ball. Some teams use aggressive punt return strategies to set up large gains or even return the punt for a touchdown.

- **Fair Catch**: If the punt returner signals for a fair catch by waving their arm overhead, they cannot be tackled but also cannot attempt to advance the ball. A fair catch is used when the coverage team is too close to allow for a safe return.

Field Goals and Extra Points

Field goals and extra points are crucial scoring plays executed by the special teams unit. These plays require precise execution and timing from multiple players.

- **Field Goals**: A field goal is an attempt to score three points by kicking the ball through the uprights of the goalpost. Field goals are typically attempted on fourth down when the offense is close enough to the goalpost but unable to score a touchdown. A reliable kicker is essential, as missed field goals waste scoring opportunities.

- **Extra Points**: After scoring a touchdown, teams have the option to kick an extra point, which is worth one point. The extra point is kicked from the 15-yard line, and it is almost automatic for professional kickers.

- **Long Snapper and Holder**: For both field goals and extra points, the long snapper plays a vital role by delivering the ball to the holder quickly and accurately. The holder must then place the ball in position for the kicker to attempt the kick.

- **Blocking**: The defending team attempts to block field goal and extra point attempts by rushing the kicker and getting a hand on the ball. A blocked field goal can swing momentum in favor of the defense.

Onside Kicks

An **onside kick** is a special type of kickoff in which the kicking team deliberately kicks the ball short, hoping to recover it before the receiving team does. This is usually a high-risk, high-reward play used when the kicking team is losing and needs to regain possession of the ball quickly.

- **Execution**: For an onside kick to be legal, the ball must travel at least 10 yards before the kicking team can recover it. Onside kicks require precision and timing, as the element of surprise is often key to their success.

- **Risk**: If the receiving team recovers the onside kick, they gain possession of the ball with excellent field position, making this a very risky tactic.

Punt and Kick Blocking

Blocking a punt or a field goal can be a game-changing moment for a defense. Special teams players rush the kicker or punter to try and block the ball before it is fully kicked.

- **Punt Block**: A punt block occurs when a defensive player reaches the punter in time to deflect or block the punt. A blocked punt can result in the ball being recovered by the defense, potentially in a position to score a touchdown.

- **Field Goal Block**: Similar to a punt block, a field goal block occurs when a defender jumps high or rushes the kicker in time to prevent the ball from crossing the uprights. Successful field goal blocks can prevent crucial points from being added to the scoreboard.

Key Special Teams Players

While special teams plays involve many players, certain positions are unique to this phase of the game. Let's take a look at the key roles in special teams.

1. **Kicker**: The kicker's main responsibilities are to kick off and attempt field goals and extra points. A strong leg, accuracy, and mental toughness are required, as kickers often perform under intense pressure.

2. **Punter**: The punter is responsible for kicking the ball on fourth down to give the defense a better field position. A good punter can pin the opposing team deep in

their territory, making it harder for them to score.

3. **Return Specialist**: This player is responsible for catching kickoffs or punts and returning them as far as possible. Return specialists must be quick, elusive, and have excellent field vision to navigate through the opposing team's coverage unit.

4. **Long Snapper**: The long snapper's job is to deliver an accurate, fast snap to the holder (for field goals and extra points) or the punter. While their role may seem minor, a bad snap can ruin a field goal or punt attempt.

5. **Gunners**: These players are responsible for sprinting down the

field during punts and kickoffs to tackle the returner. Gunners are typically some of the fastest players on the team and play a crucial role in stopping returns.

Special Teams Strategy

Special teams coaches develop detailed strategies based on the strengths and weaknesses of both their own unit and the opposing team's special teams. Key components of special teams strategy include:

1. **Kickoff Placement**: Deciding whether to kick for a touchback or aim for a spot on the field where the return team is weaker.

2. **Punt Angles**: Punting the ball toward the sideline or "coffin

corner" to limit the return team's ability to gain yards.

3. **Fake Punts and Field Goals**: Occasionally, teams will attempt a fake punt or fake field goal, where instead of kicking the ball, the punter or holder will throw or run the ball. This trick play is risky but can catch the opposing team off guard.

4. **Return Schemes**: Blocking strategies designed to open up lanes for the returner to gain maximum yardage.

Chapter 7

Developing Essential Football Skills

Success in American football hinges not only on understanding the rules and strategies but also on mastering essential skills. Whether you're a player aiming to improve your performance on the field or a fan eager to appreciate the intricacies of the game, recognizing the fundamental skills that drive success in football is crucial. This chapter will explore the key skills required for players at different positions, as well as drills and practices designed to help you develop these abilities.

Key Skills in American Football

Football encompasses a variety of skills, each tailored to specific positions on the field. While players may specialize in certain skills based on their roles, all football players benefit from developing a well-rounded skill set. The essential skills in American football can be categorized into several areas:

1. **Passing Skills**

   o **Quarterback Mechanics**: A quarterback must master the fundamental mechanics of passing, including grip, stance, footwork, and release. Proper mechanics ensure accuracy and velocity.

○ **Throwing Accuracy**: Developing the ability to throw accurately to receivers in various situations is crucial. Quarterbacks often practice throwing to targets at different distances and under varying pressure.

2. Catching Skills

○ **Hand-Eye Coordination**: Receivers, running backs, and tight ends must develop excellent hand-eye coordination to catch passes thrown in various situations, including on the run, over the shoulder, or in traffic.

- **Focus and Concentration**: Successful catching requires concentration and the ability to focus on the ball despite potential distractions, such as defenders or the crowd.

3. **Running Skills**

- **Speed and Agility**: All players benefit from speed and agility, which are crucial for evading defenders, making cuts, and sprinting to open space. Drills like cone drills and shuttle runs can enhance these skills.

- Ball Security: For running backs and receivers, securing the ball while running is essential. Players should practice holding the ball securely while running and absorbing contact.

4. Blocking Skills

- Footwork and Positioning: Offensive linemen and tight ends must master the footwork needed to establish proper blocking angles and leverage against defenders. Good positioning helps them maintain balance and power.

- o **Technique and Strength**: Developing blocking technique involves using one's body effectively to obstruct defenders while employing strength to maintain leverage during contact.

5. **Tackling Skills**

- o **Form Tackling**: Defensive players must learn the proper form for tackling to minimize the risk of injury and maximize effectiveness. This includes techniques for wrapping up the ball carrier and driving them to the ground.

- ○ **Breaking Down**: Players should practice breaking down their movements to prevent overcommitting on tackles, allowing them to adjust based on the ball carrier's actions.

6. **Kicking and Punting Skills**

- ○ **Kicking Technique**: Kickers must master the technique of kicking for both field goals and kickoffs, focusing on foot placement, follow-through, and accuracy.

- ○ **Punting Mechanics**: Punters need to develop proper punting mechanics, including the grip, drop, and follow-through, to achieve distance and hang time on their kicks.

Drills for Developing Essential Skills

Practice is key to improving your football skills. Coaches often implement specific drills to help players develop the skills outlined above. Here are some essential drills for each skill category:

Passing Drills

1. **Target Practice**: Set up targets at various distances on the field. Quarterbacks take turns throwing to these targets, focusing on accuracy and velocity. This drill

can also incorporate moving targets, such as receivers running routes.

2. **Dropback Drill**: Quarterbacks practice their dropback steps while reading defenses. This drill emphasizes footwork, timing, and decision-making under pressure.

Catching Drills

1. **Partner Toss**: Players partner up and toss the ball back and forth, gradually increasing the distance between them. This helps develop hand-eye coordination and catching skills.

2. **The JUGS Machine**: Use a JUGS machine to simulate passes thrown at various angles and speeds. This machine can help

receivers   practice   catching
difficult throws in a controlled
environment.

Running Drills

1. **Cone Drills**: Set up cones in a
   zig-zag pattern. Players sprint
   through the cones, focusing on
   quick cuts and acceleration. This
   drill   enhances   agility   and
   footwork.

2. **Ball Security Drill**: Players run
   with the football while teammates
   attempt to knock it out. This drill
   emphasizes holding onto the ball
   in the face of contact.

Blocking Drills

1. **Sled Drills**: Offensive linemen
   practice driving a blocking sled to
   develop their blocking strength

and technique. This drill focuses on maintaining low pads and proper footwork.

2. **1-on-1 Blocking**: Players take turns engaging in one-on-one blocking situations, allowing them to practice their techniques against a live opponent.

Tackling Drills

1. **Tackle Dummy Drill**: Players practice tackling techniques using a tackling dummy. This drill allows them to work on form and technique without risking injury to a teammate.

2. **Angle Tackling Drill**: Players practice pursuing a ball carrier at an angle, focusing on breaking

down and making a solid tackle while avoiding overcommitting.

Kicking and Punting Drills

1. **Kicking Tee Drill**: Kickers practice their technique using a kicking tee, focusing on accuracy and distance. This drill can include kicks from different angles and distances.

2. **Punt Returns**: Players practice catching punts while moving under pressure. This drill helps develop catching technique, decision-making, and ball security.

Incorporating Strength and Conditioning

In addition to skill development, players must also focus on strength and conditioning to excel in football. Proper conditioning enhances overall performance and reduces the risk of injury. Key aspects of strength and conditioning for football players include:

1. **Strength Training**: Incorporating weightlifting routines targeting major muscle groups can improve players' power and explosiveness on the field. Focus on compound exercises such as squats, deadlifts, and bench presses.

2. **Speed and Agility Training**: Incorporating sprinting and agility drills into your routine will help players improve their speed and

quickness, allowing them to excel in both offensive and defensive roles.

3. **Endurance Training**: Building cardiovascular endurance through running, cycling, or swimming will help players maintain their performance throughout the game, especially in late-game situations.

4. **Flexibility and Recovery**: Stretching routines and recovery strategies, including foam rolling and mobility exercises, are essential for preventing injuries and maintaining peak performance.

Chapter 8

Strategies for Beginners

Understanding and implementing strategies is crucial for success in American football, whether you're a player or a coach. While strategies can range from basic formations and plays to advanced game plans, beginners can benefit greatly from mastering fundamental concepts that lay the groundwork for their football knowledge and skills. This chapter will explore essential strategies for both offense and defense, providing beginners with a solid foundation to enhance their understanding of the game.

Understanding Offensive Strategies

The primary objective of the offense is to score points by advancing the ball into the opponent's end zone. To accomplish this, teams use a variety of offensive strategies and formations. Below are some fundamental offensive concepts that beginners should familiarize themselves with:

1. Offensive Formations

Offensive formations refer to the alignment of players on the field before the snap. Different formations dictate how the play will develop and can create advantages against the defense.

- **I Formation**: This classic formation features two running backs lined up behind the quarterback. The I formation is effective for running plays as it provides multiple blocking options. It also allows for play-action passes, where the quarterback fakes a handoff to the running back.

- **Spread Formation**: In this formation, receivers are spread out across the field, creating space for quick passes and running plays. The spread formation can force defenses to cover more ground and create mismatches with faster players.

- **Singleback Formation**: This formation has one running back and multiple wide receivers. It allows for a balance between passing and running, as the quarterback has more options and can exploit the defense's weaknesses.

2. Play Types

Once the formation is established, teams can execute various play types based on their offensive strategy. Here are some common play types:

- **Run Plays**: Run plays involve handing the ball off to a running back, who then attempts to advance the ball by running. Common types of runs include:

    - **Inside Run**: The running back runs through the tackles, utilizing blockers to gain yards.

    - **Outside Run**: The running back aims to run outside

141

the tackles, often requiring good speed and agility to evade defenders.

- **Pass Plays**: Pass plays involve the quarterback throwing the ball to a receiver. Different routes can be run depending on the design of the play, such as:

  - **Slant Route**: The receiver runs a quick diagonal route, allowing for a quick pass from the quarterback.

  - **Go Route**: The receiver sprints straight down the field, attempting to outrun defenders for a deep pass.

3. Game Situations and Strategy

Understanding game situations is vital for making strategic decisions during the game. Here are a few common scenarios:

- **Short Yardage Situations**: When only a few yards are needed for a first down, teams often rely on power running plays or short, quick passes to secure the yardage.

- **Two-Minute Drill**: In the closing moments of a game, when time is running out, teams may employ hurry-up offense strategies. This involves quick plays and no huddles to maximize scoring opportunities.

- **Red Zone Offense**: When inside the opponent's 20-yard line, the offense must focus on executing plays that can quickly result in a touchdown. This often involves a mix of short passes, runs, and strategic play calls.

Understanding Defensive Strategies

The primary goal of the defense is to prevent the offense from scoring by stopping their advances and forcing turnovers. Beginners should focus on the following defensive strategies:

1. Defensive Formations

Similar to the offense, the defense uses various formations to align their players effectively. Here are some common defensive formations:

- **4-3 Defense**: This formation includes four defensive linemen and three linebackers. It provides a solid balance against both the run and pass, allowing for flexibility in coverage and pressure.

- **3-4 Defense**: This formation features three defensive linemen and four linebackers. It is designed to create confusion for the offense and can be effective against running plays while providing coverage options.

- **Nickel Defense**: When facing a passing situation, teams may use a nickel defense, which includes five defensive backs. This formation helps defend against multiple receivers and pass-heavy offenses.

2. Defensive Responsibilities

Each player on the defense has specific responsibilities based on their position and the play being executed. Understanding these roles is crucial for effective team defense.

- **Defensive Linemen**: Their primary role is to stop the run and pressure the quarterback. Linemen must use their strength to engage blockers and create disruption in the backfield.

- **Linebackers**: Linebackers are versatile players who defend against both the run and the pass. They must read the offense quickly and react accordingly, often covering receivers or blitzing the quarterback.

- **Defensive Backs**: Defensive backs are responsible for covering receivers and preventing successful passes. They must possess speed and agility to keep up with their opponents while also being able to tackle effectively.

3. Game Situations and Strategy

Just like the offense, the defense must adapt to various game situations. Here are some common defensive strategies:

- **Prevent Defense**: In late-game situations, when the defense needs to protect against a deep pass, teams may employ a prevent defense. This strategy focuses on keeping everything in front of them to prevent big plays.

- **Blitzing**: Blitzing involves sending additional players (usually linebackers or defensive backs) to pressure the quarterback. A well-timed blitz can disrupt the offense and lead to turnovers or sacks.

- **Zone Coverage vs. Man Coverage**: Teams must decide whether to use zone coverage, where defenders cover specific areas, or man coverage, where defenders cover specific players. Each has its advantages and should be used strategically based on the opponent's strengths.

Building Your Football IQ

To truly excel at understanding and implementing strategies in football, developing your football IQ is essential. Here are some ways to enhance your knowledge and strategy application:

1. **Film Study**: Watching game film helps players and coaches analyze successful plays, formations, and defensive alignments. Understanding what works and what doesn't is key to improving strategy.

2. **Understanding Opponent Tendencies**: By analyzing opponents' game film, teams can identify patterns in their offensive and defensive strategies.

Recognizing these tendencies can help create effective game plans.

3. **Practice Situational Awareness**: During practice, create game-like situations that require quick thinking and strategic decision-making. This helps players become accustomed to adapting their strategies in real-time.

Chapter 9

How to Enjoy Watching Football

American football is more than just a sport; it's an experience that brings people together, ignites passions, and creates unforgettable memories. Whether you're a seasoned fan or a newcomer to the game, understanding how to enjoy watching football can enhance your experience. This chapter will explore various aspects of watching football, including understanding the game, creating the right atmosphere, and engaging with fellow fans, ultimately enriching your appreciation for this beloved sport.

Understanding the Game

To truly enjoy watching football, it's essential to have a grasp of the basic rules and strategies. Here's a brief overview to help you understand the game better:

1. Familiarize Yourself with the Rules

While you don't need to know every rule by heart, being aware of the key rules will enhance your viewing experience. Key points to consider include:

- **The Objective**: The primary goal of each team is to score points by advancing the ball into the opponent's end zone, either by carrying it (touchdown) or kicking it through the goalposts (field goal).

- **Scoring**: Understand how scoring works: touchdowns (6 points), extra points (1 point after touchdown), two-point conversions (2 points), and field goals (3 points).

- **Downs System**: Familiarize yourself with the concept of downs, where the offense has four attempts to gain ten yards. Understanding this system is crucial for following the progression of the game.

- **Penalties**: Learn about common penalties, such as offsides, holding, and pass interference. Knowing how these affect the game will help you understand the flow and strategy.

2. Recognize the Roles of Players

Understanding the different positions and their responsibilities will enhance your viewing experience. Here are some key positions to know:

- **Quarterback (QB)**: Often considered the leader of the offense, the quarterback is responsible for throwing passes and directing plays.

- **Running Back (RB)**: These players primarily run with the ball and can also catch passes or block for the quarterback.

- **Wide Receiver (WR)**: WRs catch passes thrown by the

quarterback and often run specific routes to get open.

- **Linebacker (LB)**: These defensive players play behind the defensive line and are involved in stopping the run and covering passes.

- **Cornerback (CB)**: Cornerbacks are tasked with covering wide receivers and preventing successful passes.

Familiarizing yourself with these positions will help you understand the dynamics of the game better.

Creating the Right Atmosphere

The environment in which you watch a football game can significantly affect your enjoyment. Here are some tips for creating the perfect atmosphere:

1. Watch with Friends and Family

Football is often best enjoyed with others. Invite friends and family over for a game day gathering. Sharing the excitement, frustrations, and triumphs of the game creates lasting memories.

2. Organize Game Day Snacks and Drinks

Food and drinks play an essential role in the game-day experience. Prepare classic football snacks such as:

- **Buffalo Wings**: Spicy, flavorful wings that are always a crowd-pleaser.

- **Chips and Dip**: A variety of dips, like salsa, guacamole, or queso, paired with tortilla chips.

- **Sliders**: Mini sandwiches filled with your choice of meat, cheese, and toppings.

- **Vegetable Platters**: Fresh veggies with dip for a healthier option.

Make sure to have plenty of beverages, including soda, beer, or cocktails, to keep everyone refreshed throughout the game.

3. Set Up a Comfortable Viewing Area

Ensure your viewing area is comfortable and conducive to watching the game. Consider the following:

- **Seating Arrangements**: Provide enough seating for all guests, whether it's couches, chairs, or floor cushions.

- **TV and Sound System**: Make sure your television is set up in a way that everyone can see clearly, and if possible, use a sound system to enhance the audio experience.

- **Lighting**: Dim the lights to create a more immersive atmosphere, similar to being in a stadium.

Engaging with the Game

To enhance your enjoyment while watching football, consider engaging with the game in various ways:

1. Follow a Team

Choosing a team to support adds a personal connection to the game. Research your team's history, roster, and players to better understand what's at stake during the season. Whether it's a local team or a national favorite, having a team to root for makes the game more exciting.

2. Learn About the Rivalries

Football is full of historic rivalries that add extra intensity to the games. Understanding the background of these matchups, including their significance and key moments, will enrich your experience and provide context to the rivalry games you watch.

3. Engage in Fantasy Football

Participating in fantasy football leagues allows you to take a more active role in the sport. By selecting real NFL players for your fantasy team, you'll be invested in multiple games and players, increasing your overall enjoyment. Fantasy leagues involve strategizing, trading, and following player performance throughout the season, making each game more exciting.

4. Utilize Technology

In today's digital age, there are various ways to enhance your viewing experience:

- **Apps and Websites**: Use sports apps to track scores, player statistics, and team standings in real time. Websites like ESPN or NFL.com offer in-depth analysis, highlights, and news updates.

- **Social Media**: Follow your favorite teams and players on social media platforms. Engaging with other fans online can provide a sense of community and enhance your excitement during games.

- **Game Highlights**: If you miss a game, watching highlights or recap videos can help you catch up and experience the excitement.

Understanding Game Analysis

Watching football goes beyond just viewing the game; it involves understanding the analysis and commentary. Familiarize yourself with the following aspects:

1. Commentary and Analysis

During the game, commentators provide insights into plays, player performance, and strategies. Listening to their analysis can enhance your understanding of the game's nuances.

2. Post-Game Analysis

After the game, take time to watch post-game analysis shows or read articles summarizing key moments, statistics, and player performances.

This will help you gain a deeper understanding of what occurred during the game and how it impacts the season.

Chapter 10

Becoming a Football Fanatic

American football is more than just a game; it's a passion that captures the hearts of millions. Becoming a football fanatic involves immersing yourself in the culture, community, and excitement surrounding the sport. Whether you're new to football or looking to deepen your connection, this chapter will explore ways to cultivate your enthusiasm and become an ardent supporter of the game.

1. Immerse Yourself in Football Culture

To truly become a football fanatic, you need to immerse yourself in the culture that surrounds the sport. Here are some ways to do that:

1.1. Learn the History of the Game

Understanding the history of American football enhances your appreciation for the sport. Dive into the origins of football, its evolution over the decades, and the key milestones that have shaped it. Here are some significant points to consider:

- **The Birth of Football**: Discover how football evolved from rugby and soccer in the late 19th century, and how the formation of the National Football League (NFL) in 1920 marked the beginning of professional football as we know it today.

- **Legendary Moments**: Familiarize yourself with iconic moments in football history, such as memorable Super Bowl games, record-breaking performances, and significant rule changes.

- **Hall of Fame Players**: Learn about legendary players and coaches who have left an indelible mark on the game, such as Jim Brown, Jerry Rice, Tom Brady, and Bill Belichick.

1.2. Engage with Football Media

Follow football-related media to stay informed and connected with the sport:

- **Podcasts**: Listen to football podcasts that cover game analysis, player interviews, and discussions about current events in the NFL. Some popular ones include "The Bill Simmons Podcast," "Pardon My Take," and "Around the NFL."

- **Television Shows**: Tune in to shows like "NFL Total Access" and "Monday Night Countdown" for highlights, analysis, and commentary on games and players.

- **Documentaries and Films**: Watch documentaries and films that explore the history and culture of football, such as "The Last Dance," "Friday Night

Lights," or "Remember the Titans."

1.3. Read Books About Football

Books about football can provide valuable insights into the sport, its players, and its strategies. Consider reading:

- **Autobiographies and Biographies**: Explore the lives of legendary players and coaches through their stories. Books like "I Am Third" by Gale Sayers and "Belichick: The Making of the Greatest Football Coach of All Time" by Ian O'Connor offer personal perspectives on the game.

- **Football Strategy Books**: Gain a deeper understanding of the game by reading about its strategies and tactics. Books like "The New Thinking Man's Guide to Pro Football" by Paul Zimmerman and "Football 101: The NFL's Guide for New Fans" by John R. Davis can help you grasp the intricacies of the game.

2. Join the Football Community

Connecting with other fans is a vital part of becoming a football fanatic. Here's how to engage with the football community:

2.1. Attend Live Games

Nothing compares to the excitement of being at a live football game. Here are some tips for attending games:

- **Home Games**: Support your local team by attending home games. Experience the atmosphere of the stadium, cheer for your team, and enjoy the camaraderie of fellow fans.

- **Tailgating**: Join in on tailgating festivities before the game. This pre-game tradition involves grilling, sharing food, and socializing with other fans in the parking lot. It's a great way to bond with fellow supporters.

- **Away Games**: Consider traveling to see your team play on the road. This can be an exciting adventure, allowing you to explore new cities while cheering for your team.

2.2. Join Fan Clubs and Online Communities

Becoming part of a fan club or online community can deepen your connection to the sport. Look for:

- **Local Fan Clubs**: Many NFL teams have local fan clubs that organize watch parties, events, and community service. Join these clubs to meet like-minded individuals who share your passion.

- **Online Forums and Social Media**: Engage with fans on platforms like Reddit, Facebook, and Twitter. Participate in discussions, share opinions, and connect with others who share your enthusiasm for football.

3. Master the Art of Game Day Experience

Game day is an event that brings fans together, and mastering the experience can elevate your enthusiasm. Here are some strategies:

3.1. Create a Game Day Ritual

Developing a personal game day ritual can make each game feel special. Consider these ideas:

- **Dress the Part**: Wear your favorite team's gear, whether it's a jersey, hat, or face paint. Dressing up shows your support and helps create a festive atmosphere.

- **Pre-Game Traditions**: Establish rituals that you perform before each game, such as cooking a specific dish, listening to team-themed music, or watching highlight reels.

3.2. Host Game Day Parties

Share your enthusiasm by hosting friends and family for game day gatherings. Here are tips for hosting:

- **Themed Decor**: Decorate your space with team colors, banners, and memorabilia to create a vibrant environment.

- **Activities and Games**: Organize activities like football trivia, prop bets, or a squares game to keep guests engaged during the game.

- **Invite Guests**: Encourage friends and family to wear their team gear and create a lively atmosphere filled with excitement and camaraderie.

4. Participate in Fantasy Football

Participating in fantasy football can significantly enhance your engagement with the sport. Here's how to get started:

4.1. Join a Fantasy League

Find a league to join, whether it's with friends, family, or online communities. Fantasy leagues typically draft players from the NFL, and you compete based on their performance throughout the season.

4.2. Understand the Scoring System

Each league may have a different scoring system, so familiarize yourself with how points are awarded. This knowledge will help you make informed decisions during your draft and weekly lineups.

4.3. Stay Informed on Player Performances

Keep track of player statistics, injuries, and matchups. Utilize fantasy football apps and websites to help manage your team, make trades, and adjust your lineup.

5. Embrace the Passion of Rivalries

Football is full of intense rivalries that add excitement and depth to the game. Here's how to embrace this aspect:

5.1. Understand Rivalry Matchups

Research historic rivalries within the NFL, such as:

- **Dallas Cowboys vs. Washington Commanders**: One of the oldest and most storied rivalries in football, known for its fierce competition.

- **Green Bay Packers vs. Chicago Bears**: The NFL's oldest rivalry, steeped in tradition and intensity.

- **New England Patriots vs. New York Jets**: Known for its passionate fan bases and competitive matchups, this rivalry brings extra excitement to every meeting.

Understanding these rivalries adds context and significance to games, making them even more thrilling to watch.

5.2. Celebrate Rivalry Games

When rivalry games are on the schedule, treat them as special events. Host parties, engage in friendly banter with fans of opposing teams, and enjoy the heightened emotions these games bring.

Conclusion

As we conclude this comprehensive guide to American football for beginners, it's essential to reflect on the journey you've taken through the fascinating world of this beloved sport. From understanding the basics of the game to developing essential skills, exploring strategies, and learning how to enjoy the game as a fan, you've gained a wealth of knowledge that will enhance your experience, whether you're playing or watching.

Embracing the Game

American football is not just about touchdowns and tackles; it's a rich tapestry of strategy, teamwork, and passion. By learning the rules, the roles of players, and the intricacies of the field, you've equipped yourself with the tools to appreciate the game on a deeper level. Understanding the dynamics of offense and defense, as well as special teams, allows you to recognize the skill and preparation that go into each play.

Moreover, developing essential football skills prepares you for a more active role in the sport. Whether you're tossing a football with friends, participating in a local league, or simply enjoying a casual game, the skills you've learned can be applied on the field.

The Joy of Community and Camaraderie

One of the most rewarding aspects of football is its ability to bring people together. As you embrace your passion for the game, you will find camaraderie with fellow fans and players. Engaging in community events, attending live games, or participating in fantasy leagues creates lasting connections that enhance your enjoyment of the sport.

Becoming a football fanatic opens doors to new friendships and shared experiences, whether through game-day gatherings, rivalries, or spirited discussions about your favorite teams and players. The sense of belonging to a community of passionate fans is a significant part of the joy that football brings.

Looking Ahead

As you embark on your journey as a football enthusiast, remember that the landscape of the sport is always evolving. New strategies, emerging talents, and innovative technologies are shaping the future of football. Embrace these changes and continue to seek out knowledge, whether through media, literature, or engaging with fellow fans.

Stay curious and open-minded as you explore different aspects of the game. Whether it's diving deeper into advanced strategies, following the latest trends in player performance, or simply enjoying the thrill of a game day with friends, there's always more to discover.

Final Thoughts

Football is more than just a game; it's a celebration of athleticism, strategy, and community. It embodies the spirit of competition, the joy of teamwork, and the thrill of victory. As you continue your journey in understanding and enjoying American football, carry with you the passion and excitement that the sport evokes.

We hope this guide has inspired you to explore, engage, and fully enjoy the world of American football. Whether you're cheering from the stands, discussing strategies with friends, or playing on the field, may your love for the game grow deeper with each experience. Welcome to the exhilarating world of football—where every game is a new opportunity for excitement, connection, and unforgettable memories.

Printed in Great Britain
by Amazon